D1636471

Illustrated by: Jonathan Lane

Author: Jatali Bellanton

Summary:

"It is the first day of summer break and all Ari and his friends can think and talk about is the new game console to be released in one month.

At a price point of $550, their parents have refused to purchase it for them so the kids have taken it upon themselves to just earn it on their own...

In this first edition amongst the lessons, they start to learn are concepts like the barter system, depreciation, using one's skills to generate income and wants vs needs."

Ages: 8-17

Provided by Publisher.

ISBN-10: 0-692-80200-2 / ISBN-13: 978-0692802007

<u>To be coordinated with the power of balance, your mind and your temple must be running parallel</u>.

<u>Peter Tosh</u>

INTRO

Journal Entry #1 -Ari's thoughts:

Imagine there is an entrance, walk through it and now it appears as if you have just entered an empty room.

Once in the room, the door closes swiftly behind you and it has disappeared. DO NOT PANIC, remain calm, breathe in, breathe out and just remember when you are ready to you can either create a new exit or find a pre-existent hidden door. So for now just enjoy the peace and calm this empty room possesses. You are now relaxed and free of all self-doubt and negativity.

My nightly meditations start with this thought every day or so. It is a staple scenario my parents used to whisper to me when they were teaching me how to clear my mind and meditate.

You see as a child the realm of my possibilities are endless and so are yours.

WELCOME TO A PART OF MY WORLD.

If you have no confidence in self, you are twice defeated in the race of life.

<u>Marcus Garvey</u>

CHAPTER ONE

WEDNESDAY

My name is Arionne Folami, my father is Nigerian and my mother was born in the U.K. to African immigrants (Cape Verdean). They met during their undergrad studies at a University in England and somehow their roads led them here to the USA, New York to be specific, where I was born.

To the outside world I am seen as a teenage boy with bright brown eyes (and wrapped in skin that can best be described as having a bronzish, terracotta complexion), who has a big curly fro; and to my friends, a 13yr old who has just completed the 9th grade, a person great with money and known by the nickname "Ari the Motivator". If you ask me about myself, I would tell you I am just an ever-evolving being who is here to learn, expand and elevate.

Thus far in my life I have had many moments where I had to rise above a challenge or prove to myself that I can do it on my own without asking - I mean, there is nothing wrong with asking for help, it is just not my first go to. Some might voice the opinion that I am too young - why don't I just ask my parents off the bat, but even at this "young" age I feel as if they have given me enough discernment to accomplish many tasks and to know when I actually need backup.

Oh boy, it is 10:30 pm and I am exhausted. Tomorrow is the first day of summer break and I have a full day ahead of me.

In the midst of chaos, there is also opportunity.

<u>Sun Tzu</u>

CHAPTER TWO

THURSDAY

Today is going to go down in my journal as a great day. Not just because it is going to be a high of 92°F, but because it is officially the first day of summer break. As a tradition, both the middle school and high school kids all go to the playground located equidistant from both schools.

I am still close friends with the kids from my old middle school and have made new ones at my current high school, so I'm definitely looking forward to seeing both groups in one place. Today's goal amongst my group of friends is to come up with a way to make $550 each. You may be wondering why we need so much money - Well, in one month and two days a new video game console named " VR Station" will be released onto the market, and by the ads, we all think it is going to be the best one yet. It is supposed to integrate the best features from all of the competitors in the market into one console and exceed them. The console will include some virtual reality headsets and a slew of other cutting-edge features.

I am usually the go-to person in my group when it comes to "get-rich" ideas or basic financial questions since it is no secret that both of my parents have made it onto the Forbes top 100 list of rich and successful power couples.

As I walk into the park I notice that all of the gamers are excitedly discussing the new console and how badly most of them wanted or thought they needed it. It always got to me when I heard people say they needed a game as if it was a true necessity and their world would end if they did not receive it.

BINGO! I spot my group of friends sitting at our favorite picnic table and head over. We are split between three middle school kids (Parry, Julie and Jasper) and five of us from the High School (Courtney, Tanya, Lincoln, Mercedes and me).

Within minutes of our debriefing, I realize that only my friend Julie and I have the money to purchase the console even if it came out tomorrow, but the rest of the team - did not have the same luxury. Most of their parents told them NO WAY!

Parry, Jasper, and Tanya's parents said they refused to put any money towards a game they would probably barely play with, they all shared a track record of showing a lack of interest in their toys within three months of ownership.

Courtney, Mercedes and Julie's parents simply said no without explanations, and Lincoln's parents were not too thrilled with his mistreatment of the last game they purchased him and said they would think about it. For him, that could easily be changed to a yes with good behavior, but the only question was if he would get the money within a month.

Anyways, being the optimist that I am, I started formulating a plan and threw it out there. My words were: "Let's create a challenge. Why don't we all earn the money on our own without expecting it from our parents, or using any of our savings? If we can earn the money within the month then we have the option of buying the game console or not".

We all have different strengths and weaknesses so I offered to work with all of the people in our crew, and thus our journey has started.

I would help guide everyone for at least one day with the understanding anyone who earned at least $100 in excess profit following my tips and tricks would pay me $60. I would then put in the difference with the money I will be earning from my paid internship, which I start on Monday, to reach my goals.

Whatever it is you're seeking won't come in the form you're expecting.

<u>**Haruki Murakami**</u>

CHAPTER THREE

MONDAY - WEEK ONE

It is the first official week of the challenge and I am on my way to meet up with JuJu. His real name is Parry Xavier but since people always seem to mess up or have jokes on his first name, he prefers to introduce himself using his nickname JuJu, which was given to him by his favorite uncle. In case you were wondering what was so funny about the name Parry, well that word is slang for the word friend in Jamaican patois.

Juju and I have been friends since he emigrated from Kingston, Jamaica with his parents about 7 years ago at the age of six. His dad got a job here in NY one month into the school year, so he came to my class later than everyone else, but we instantly clicked because he was very sarcastic and reminded me of one of my cousins from England.

The story goes: Our teacher asked us to come to the front of the classroom and tell everyone what we wanted to be when we grew up, and Parry's response was that he was already living his dream as a chef. Everyone laughed but I knew he was serious, and it was solidified when I noticed that during lunch time he had no interest in junk food and had a well-presented meal in his lunchbox. When I asked him his favorite dish he mentioned dishes from all over the world and I knew then that he was officially cool (btw, I know it might sound cliche but he really is from an area called Spanish Town in Kingston Jamaica).

Back to the challenge: Parry's situation was a little different than the others' in the sense that like me, he had a designated summer job. He was working at a restaurant as a dishwasher where he was able to learn more tricks of the trade. He would not have time to do anything too physical or take on another job. His current one was five days a week, and he already made a promise to himself to donate half of his check to a charity back in Jamaica, and to save the other half of it - minus the money he needed for transportation to and from work. He did not want to go back on his word even though it was a personal wager.

We came to the conclusion that his best course of action would be to either sell a bunch of his small items until he reached his goal or a few big ticket items which would help him attain his goal more quickly.

Step 1 would be to decide which toys he would want to sell. Step 2 was to research how much he could get for the items on various websites and forums. Step 3 - Once he decided upon what he was going to sell he had to ask his parents for permission to sell them, and step 4 would be to list them for sale on various websites and forums at a reasonable price.

Once in his house, we went straight to the game room which was located in the basement. His parents had a pool table in there but I think every other toy in that room belongs to JuJu.

We started out by putting all of the toys he no longer played with to one side of the room, leaving the ones he wanted to keep in their designated places. Despite the hundreds of toys he had, it was hard for him to part with a majority of them due to their sentimental value, so our lineup was not looking too great. I grabbed his laptop and began doing some online research on the general values of the second-hand items he ended up choosing and realized they were not going to bring in enough money. We had six stuffed animals worth about $20 for all 6, some lettered play mat flooring with all of its pieces in great condition for about $25, a set of wooden blocks that, surprisingly, could potentially fetch $30, a set of Legos worth maybe $15, and his best item - an old hand-held Nintendo which was now worth $50.
As you can see that means in an optimal situation it would only get him $170, and that leaves him with a whole lot more to go.

Now we were back to square one and I was starting to feel like this was a hopeless case, then - EUREKA!!! JuJu jumped up and started to run towards what he was calling his console closet. I had no idea what he was talking about but apparently right next to the bathroom what I thought was a supply closet like in my house ended up being where they stored all of the game consoles they owned. There was everything from an original Atari to a Sega Genesis and the latest

Wii. Out of the stack in front of us, JuJu owned two PlayStation consoles, two Xbox consoles and two Wii's.

JACKPOT! This should definitely be worth more than enough. In fact, I think by selling just one PlayStation and a couple of smaller items he should have enough. JuJu was telling me his dad paid about $450 for his PlayStation so we were initially elated, but little did we realize that depreciation would be a major issue. He decided upon selling his PS3 first so we ran to the computer and upon investigation were hit with the harsh reality that in 10 years it depreciated significantly, and was only worth maybe $200. We then ran the ps4 into the cyber world and although it was only 3 years old, it was worth only $270 used and $300 new.

Ouch! We now started to wonder if this loss in value was strictly a PlayStation issue but after looking up the XBox and Wii we came across the same kind of results. This left JuJu in a conundrum: Did it even make sense to purchase another console ever again at full price?

Well, for now, he decided he wanted to only list a Wii, his Xbox One and a Playstation3. He knew if at any point he wanted them back he could probably just repurchase them. As well, he wanted to donate the smaller items to a charity here in New York.

Now that we knew what he wanted to list we just had to make sure his parents did not mind.

We found both his mom and dad in the kitchen making breakfast. We told them about selling the consoles so he could purchase the new VR Station that would be corning out in a month and also expressed his interest in donating the other toys. They both loved the ideas and thought they were amazing. That put us both at ease, then right on cue as if she read my mind, JuJu's mother - who still had a slight Jamaican accent, asked me if I would like to have breakfast with them. You should already know I said YES! She made my favorite: Ackee and saltfish with sweet plantain, fried dumplings, yams and bammy. How could I say no?

After breakfast, I helped JuJu list his games on various sites and social media pages, then headed on my way. In total, he had the potential to make $750 if no one decided to haggle with him.

With that accomplished, I was now off to my paid internship at a local news station. I had noticed that they put an ad out for a paid teen intern last summer and I nervously submitted. I kicked all of that nervousness to the side during my first interview and nailed it and was hired for the summer part-time position. Every business day between 11 am - 4 pm I was an assistant to the head director of sales.

Choose a job you love, and you will never have to work a day in your life.

<u>Confucius</u>

CHAPTER4

FRIDAY - WEEK ONE

Day four and I've just finished a jog with my parents and I am filling them in on my missions for the day: First, to meet with Mercedes over at Courtney's house and second, to head over to my internship.

This time last year they both volunteered to read and play with sick kids at a local hospital and said they enjoyed it very much. This is the reason why I want to pair them together for this project, plus they have in two separate conversations hinted towards the fact that they would like to do something with younger kids which jogged my thoughts as to how they can make money while spending time with kids.

This plan would involve them doing just that so I figured - what better way for Mercedes who is 15 yrs old, and Courtney who's 16 yrs old, to spend the summer and make money than to in some way shape or form to babysit.

I decided to ride my bicycle over to Courtney's house since I was a little tired from this mornings' jog and the bonus would be that I could then ride from her house to my job. My dad told me he would pick me up after work and I was looking forward to it. I definitely would not want to ride my bike all the way from my job to my house.

As I pulled up to Courtney's house I headed to the back porch where she told me they would be having breakfast with her mom (Ms. Donovan). Courtney was born here in New York but her mom was born and raised in Ireland. They both had fiery red hair and spoke pretty quickly. Something I found fascinating about Courtney is that she had a slight Irish accent from all of her visits to Ireland and from living with a mom who's accent was thick.

As I get closer I can smell colcannon (a dish of mashed potatoes and cabbage that was scrumptious) and hear laughter. Listening to their cheery voices make me think about how excited they were when I called to ask them if they would like to team up.

After greetings, Mercedes could barely hide her excitement and told me that they did not spill the beans and wanted to give me the honor of telling Ms. Donovan about our idea and in what way we would like to have her help.

The details: they would open up a babysitters club at the house, specifically targeting parents who attend the gym nearby that needed a place to bring their kids -A "gym care fun zone" in a sense, where parents could go to the gym to work out for one hour at a time and have the convenience of dropping their kids off at a safe, nearby location. It would go by the name: CM Sitters.

Since Courtney and Mercedes wanted to have temporary jobs as a fail-safe, we worked the hours out to be off hours when most daycare centers nearby were closed, such as on Friday afternoons and on the weekends, in order to avoid eating away at the profits of other local daycare businesses. The biggest advantages of their fun zone would be that Courtney's house is literally across the street from the gym, there would be cameras set up so parents can log in and see what their kid(s) are up to. The best part was that if Courtney's mom agreed to it, that since she is a registered nurse we would only schedule kids for when she is home and advertise the service as having an RN on site - a huge selling point!

Ms. Donovan was so proud of us that she not only agreed to help with the kids but to help baby proof the family room, help drive us around as we distributed flyers, give us $50 towards baby proofing items, purchasing some basic kid educational toys and whatever additional knickknacks we needed.

Now that we had Ms. Donovan's schedule we started to go over particulars.

The hours of operation would be Fridays 5pm-9pm, Saturdays: 10am-6pm and Sundays: 12pm-4pm. They would babysit only 4 kids per hour, it would cost $15/hr per kid, and the ages we were targeting would be 5yrs old - 9yrs old.

We then proceeded to prepare the family room for the kids since it was the largest room on the first floor, had a door leading to the backyard and another door alongside the TV which leads to a bathroom in the comer. We brought up the mini fridge from the basement so we would technically never have to leave the room and once satisfied all we had to do now was create the flyers and get the wifi cameras from Mercedes house.

We asked permission to hang the flyer in the gym, nearby stores and the Laundromat. Within 1 hour we started to receive calls and booking parents.

At this point, it was looking like they would make their goal amount within two weekends. All parents had to leave a deposit which would be non-refundable at least one day in advance and in order to not exchange cash with anyone Courtney had the great idea of using an app her mom normally uses to transfer her allowance to her because the money was available instantly without incurring any fees, and there were multiple accounts it could be transferred to.

We created invoice templates and since they were both owners of bank accounts, set up the account so that each payment would pool and by Sunday night of each week, they would split their profits down the middle.

We had two more hours together before I headed to work so Ms. Donovan brought us to Mercedes' house which was only 5 blocks away so that she could run in and get all 6 of her wifi cameras.

The reason she owned them was because last year her father

surprised her with a trip to visit Cuba, which was where he was from, but told her that she would not be allowed to bring her cat with them and although they hired a cat sitter she wanted to be able to log on and see her cat Ms. Fluffy at any time.

She did the research and found a system which would allow her to log on whenever she wanted and have visuals of Ms. Fluffy in any room she was in. Ironically once they arrived in Cuba between seeing all of the beautiful architecture, old cars, spending time on a gorgeous beach named Playa Pilar and swimming with dolphins in an area named Varadero she ended up barely checking up on Ms. Fluffy. I remember the pictures from that trip like it was yesterday.

She might not have used them much back then but this was going to be a great asset to their business now. A feature which made the cameras the coolest was that they would allow us to provide the parents with a code enabling them to view their kids while they were at the gym.

Each hour and day the code would change in order to increase the security of who could view the kids and limit it only to the parents who in that particular hour had a child on the premise.

Mercedes' father was also a single parent and was at work so she was in and out quickly and within 15 minutes the video system was all set up.

We created the invoices for the parents who called to schedule appointments, and two calendars - one in a daily calendar notebook, and the other on the computer where we not only kept track of all of the kids who were scheduled but also attached notes in regards to their favorite games, foods, sensitivities, tips to keep them happy, comfort items they might need and any allergies they may have.

In a little over half of a day, we were able to basically set everything up since there were four of us on deck helping out, and we booked many slots for the whole weekend which totaled $375 - and the day was not even over yet!

With four more weekends to go, I could tell they were on their way to having a very profitable business and easily make their goal with little to no problems.

When you have mastered numbers, you will in fact no longer be reading numbers, any more than you read words when reading books you will be reading meanings.

W. E. B. Du Bois

CHAPTER FIVE

SATURDAY - WEEK ONE

Phew! It is the day after I met up with Mercedes and Courtney, and I am just relaxing this morning and staying in to look over my notes and lessons from my boss/mentor over at my internship.

She mentioned a few things which would be a topic of discussion for me to ask my parents about.

One of those topics was in regards to credit scores and how they affect the APR's of credit cards and various forms of debt and compounding interest.

This was a category I knew little to nothing about prior to this week. It came into play because on one of the days I was in the office working, my mentor's daughter Audrey came in crying because she maxed out her credit card the previous month and then lost her job this month and could afford to pay even the minimum bill.

Audrey was very irresponsible with money and at the age of 19 years old, and against her mother's better judgment, she opened a card with a credit line of $5000 and an APR of 20% for supposed emergencies. Things went left when she put down a deposit on a car which totaled

$3500 and then charged a few of the monthly bills on her card while paying the minimum requirement. Before she knew it her card was maxed out.

Here is what I learned:
Credit Cards were loans given to people which normally had interest rates tacked on with the understanding you could purchase what you wanted within the limit of the card and be given time to pay it off. Interest is what you pay the lender for the loan if you don't pay the balance in full each month and can be a higher or lower amount depending on your credit score.
A credit score is a system which is used in some countries by lenders to rate how responsible you are with money via numbers ranging from the lowest 300 to a high of 900 and impacts your APR.
APR stands for Annual Percentage Rate which is the yearly rate of interest.

The way it works is if you purchase items with monthly payments as you pay them off on time or in advance your score rises because you have displayed you can be trusted with money.

The longer you pay particular bills on time - the higher the score goes and the more trustworthy lenders will know you to be, thus be willing to lend you more money or give you better deals such as a low APR vs a high one...

In a way looking at the trends I get the feeling they make the APR high and make it harder for people with bad credit to make purchases as a deterrent for people to be mindful of their financial choices and know the benefits of paying on time.

This can all be good or bad in some situations.

ARE YOU WITH ME THUS FAR?

Just in case I will explain this concept in a different way: Imagine I lend you $1000 at an APR of 10% and give you a minimum monthly payment of 1% your minimum monthly payment would be $15 and at that rate it would take you 8 years and 1 month to pay me back and I would've made $1,465.74 total although you only borrowed $1,000 in the beginning.

The worst part was due to compounding interest depending her rate if you don't pay off your card in 12 months that amount would jump even higher.

I do not know about you but when or if I ever get a credit card I am going to first make sure I have good credit sense and be very wise about what kind of deal I sign up for all the while using it wisely.

Those 3 digits ranging from 300 to 900, no matter how much money you have in the bank, could mean the difference between paying more or less for an item rather it is one day buying a home, or something as little as charging something on a credit card.

Good credit can also help you be rewarded for being financially responsible.

Anyways now that I have recapped a little glimpse into what I have learned today I must now get ready for my next day in the office. We are supposed to discuss Stocks, bonds, penny stocks, IPO's, etc...

HAVE I MENTIONED THAT I LOVE MY INTERNSHIP?

Art must discover and reveal the beauty which prejudice and caricature have overlaid.

<u>Alain LeRoy Locke</u>

CHAPTER SIX

MONDAY - WEEK TWO

Three team members down and four more to go. Things with everyone on our team are looking good thus far and I am getting better at managing my time.

I am currently sitting with Fatima in her backyard as she helps the babysitter look after her younger siblings. I should probably fill you in a little:

I can say that although she is the youngest in our group at the age of 11 yrs. Old, Fatima is possibly smart enough to be attending my high school but her parents did not want her to skip grades and she was happy for now, being with kids in her own age group.

As I listed some options for her to potentially make her console money in one month, I was met with many "no ways" and had to go back to the drawing board. NO! TO BAKE-OFFS, NO! TO WASHING CARS, NO! TO BEING A DOG WALKER, NO!, NO!, NO!

I mean at this point I was starting to give up hope that I would figure it out. I haven't been this stumped yet so I asked her to give me a sec and started to clear my mind.

As I did this Julie pulled out a little box full of beads and started to decorate her hijab, A hijab is a head wrap worn by girls in her culture. Oh, have I mentioned that Fatima is Muslim? She is from a traditional Muslim household and as such when she started puberty started to wear a hijab.

Up until the day, I saw her wearing one I never knew its name, importance, or significance. I thought it was something like what nuns wore and I remember the first time she came to school with it on we were all inquisitive and asked a ton of questions. Some of the kids were taken aback at first and started to act a little funny around her but the more questions she answered the more things got back to normal even with them.

Fatima is not shy at all and is so funny that not only did we learn a little about her culture but she also had us laughing a few times along the way. In one story she said the first time wearing one it was 90°F outside and she thought she was going to melt into a puddle. Lol.

Funny enough, I tend to forget it is even there because I see it so often and hers are always colorful, glittery reflections of her personality. Suddenly I realized that here she was in front of me putting little rhinestones all over another hijab she owns manually. I always thought she purchased them with the designs on them already but I now knew she is usually the one to do all of her own designs (do you see where I am going with this?) and now I had to ask her some questions:

Question #1:
How many Hijabs can you design in one day/ one week?
Question#2:
About how much does it cost to make one, including cloth?
Question#3:
How much would she spend on a decorated hijab like the ones she wears?

Once Julie realized where I was headed with my questions she was so excited that she was speaking too quickly for me to even keep up with her.

The slower version was that it takes her 20 minutes to make one hijab and she has in the past comfortably made eight of them in one day using a sewing machine as well as hand beading designs.

Overall the materials cost $10 for thread and cloth worst case scenario and she even knew of a market which sold hijabs, stones and jewels. At the market, they sold basic designs for $20 and an average of $45 for the more intricate designs.

The biggest issue was that the market was only open on the weekends but she could call the lady who organized it and asked how much they would charge her to have her own section to sell all of the hijabs. While she looked for the woman's number I did some research on my computer and came across websites which had them for sale and realized her price points were accurate.

I asked her what name would she use for her business if she opened up a clothing store or line and she said she liked the name Sparkled Hijab, so I went to the government's website to see if they had that name available. It was open and I knew that Fatima had enough money for start-up Capital which in this case was $30 if she filed for it herself. The plan was to legitimize her business at first as a DBA, that acronym stood for " Doing Business As", and it was just to get her feet wet since she might want to continue this business even after she accomplished her challenge.

Fatima and I went inside to ask her parents for permission and let them in on her plan. Her dad was a lawyer who specialized in patents. Patents are a way people protected their inventions. Not only did her father love the idea but he even offered to pay for her DBA and file it for her.

It was at that point Fatima asked her dad why he never taught her about a DBA as a way of doing business. Never did I imagine when I mentioned a DBA to her that she wouldn't know what that was; you see her father used to set up peoples' corporations for them and had tons of books in their family den on the topic. I remember he once told us the story of how he got started right after graduating - by legitimizing companies by setting up LLC's, C-Corps, S-Corps, Trademarking and copyrights before settling on patent law.

Fatima's dad told her that he thought she would think of it all as boring stuff and would have taught her about it when she was a little bit older. Boy oh boy was he ever wrong. He then reminded Fatima that she should practice good business protocols like paying sales tax and logging all income, etc...

We both thought it was a great idea and started to look into good accounting programs at which point her father mentioned he had one he normally utilized for personal business and could create a separate account for her new startup.

He also agreed to bring her shopping for supplies and to the bank to create a new account for her so that she could have direct access to her earnings and put them all in one place. Just as they were headed out the door the woman from the market called and told her she would give her the space for $50 compared to the $300 everyone else paid for her ingenuity. It would be for all day on Saturday and Sunday, the woman could not stop saying how impressed she was that such a young girl was interested in starting a business. With her dad in her corner and everything on track, I knew my job here was done.

En route to the fabric store, Fatima called me to share that she was thinking of ideas for her next designer hijabs, and she would make a couple that were the same basic pattern but that each one would have a unique style.

As I was at my internship and taking a mini lunch break I noticed texts from Fatima saying her dad applied for the DBA and she had her own bank account. She said she also started to design as well and sent out a blast email with the first samples as teasers to all of her friends and relatives with a note that if they wanted to purchase it that they could in person at the market this upcoming Saturday and Sunday.

It made me happy to have yet another person excited to be doing something that they love and could not wait to see how her sales would go.

After work, I headed home where my parents were both waiting for me. It was very big in my home to eat dinner as a family. During dinner, my cell phone started to ring but I had to silence it because it was a big NO-NO to even look at mobile devices during dinner time.

I told my parents about how our pursuits were coming along and my dad and mom suggested that I started my own consulting firm. The way things were going I was starting to seriously think about it.

On my way to my room to watch some TV I checked to see who called me and I realized it was Lincoln. Lincoln out of all of us was the most musically gifted person in our circle. I say this because he knew how to play four instruments and has studied them in other countries.

He was born and raised in Colorado but his dad who is another successful entrepreneur amongst the parents acquired a major hedge fund here in New York four years ago and they moved here a year later but Lincoln blended right in with us.

Anyways, I called him back and he proceeded to tell me that he was creating flyers and his business idea was to fix broken toys as well as put an ad in a local newspaper to teach kids younger than himself how to play the violin and cello since those were two of his favorite instruments. Since he is both very handy and good at music I told him it was a great idea and started to voice my concerns but he did not want to hear them and said he was busy.

Oh well, I tried so that's just left me with one less person to focus on in the group.

On second thought I am quite tired. I am going to play some music and go to sleep instead.

With Lincoln confident he had his money makers, that would leave Jasper and Tanya who I know both started little things but were not feeling like they were making enough money.

The best work is not what is most difficult for you; it is what you do best.

<u>Jean-Paul Sartre</u>

CHAPTER SEVEN

WEDNESDAY - WEEK TWO

Nearing the end of another week and today Jasper and I have to cross paths. Jasper's family is Japanese and he has a unique steelo. Some days you will find him wearing traditional garb and others in a leather biker jacket full of studs.

I remember the first time I ever went to Jasper's house I automatically started to take off my shoes before I entered and his parents were impressed. When his dad mentioned that he was impressed that I did my homework on his culture in regards to the shoes I thought it only fair to let him know that it was second nature to me because it was common to not bring outside shoes into the household in my culture as well.

That was also the first day I ever tried wasabi. Have you ever tried wasabi? It is a green sauce which in my opinion looks like a mashed up avocado. With a warning from Jasper in regards to its spiciness, I sampled a little drop and still remembered thinking that my mouth was on fire.

So many good memories have been shared with all of my friends that it is hard to imagine that this is only the beginning part of our lives. It is actually why I have started to log my thoughts in a journal.

Well, today I have invited Jasper to meet up with me after my swimming lessons because I know he looks for excuses to come here. People think that I am a great swimmer until they see Jasper swim. He has mentioned confidently that one day he will swim in the Olympics and I believe that not only will it happen but he will also win a gold medal.

I was currently entering the area where we agreed to meet and I could tell he was already here. How? Well, since I've known Jasper he has always attracted crowds while he swims and as I enter I can hear a group of kids saying things like they wish they could swim like him.

Sure enough, as I got to the end I could see him doing laps like a fish, cutting thru the water quickly.

Once Jasper popped up for some air he noticed me and headed to the end to jump out. After we greeted each other I asked him if he tried out for the Lifeguard job that was posted on the bulletin board or has he given any thought to training kids to swim. I mean seriously, they were all just there watching him, but he reminded me that he does not have the patience to teach anyone.

Within 3 seconds and bursting with excitement he described his amazing idea and what he would need to execute it.

As we sat on the bleachers he went into details on how he started to sweep the front of a local store before business hours for $15 and after doing it for two days straight he had a business owner on the block approach him about doing theirs as well.

After that, he went and asked all ten of the stores and boutiques on the block if they would be interested and all ten of them said yes. He would sweep their front or back entrances once a day and scheduled it for Monday, Friday and Saturday schedule.

Now his biggest issue was the fact that more stores would like his cleaning services and not only is he currently a one-man team but some of the areas would be a hassle to go to on a regular basis.

He and I both agreed he needed other people to help him succeed in this scenario and this is where I could possibly help. He wanted to know if I knew anyone and I jumped right on it and started to make calls right there inside the gymnasium. My first thought was Tanya.

I got Tanya on the phone and explained that Jasper was going to keep a percentage of all payments raised since he found the jobs. Not only was that fine with her but she asked if we needed other people because her brother Nelson who was a freshman in college, needed a job and had a car. Jasper and I said bring him at the same time with big grins on our faces.

I thought for sure Tanya's money maker was going to involve cooking in some way but this was an equally good opportunity and I know that she is very tidy from playing over at her house a few times.

Did I mention that Tanya is another chef in our group? In fact last year December she won a very popular kid cooking show by displaying fusions of her mixed heritage in each dish. Her father is 1st generation Haitian American and owns a very successful Caribbean restaurant and her mother's family is from Washington D.C. as far back as she could trace her genealogy and teaches at a local school. To celebrate after she won the show, her parents invited all of our families over for Soup Joumou (a pumpkin/squash soup full of spices, vegetables and flavors which I could eat three bowls of back to back) on New Year's day. Soup Joumou was a tradition which honored Haiti's independence day which her dad cooked every year in remembrance of it, but this year Tanya was the chef and her dad was the sous chef.

Thirty minutes later Tanya arrived with Nelson alongside her. Her brother is very cool and even offered to pick up others who needed to be dropped off to work as well on his route without an additional cost.

Within one hour of returning missed calls, Jasper had sixty storefronts to clean in an eight-block radius. Fifty stores at $15 each and ten for $25 each because they were so big.

We were going to need additional workers so we all made a few more calls and between Jasper, Tanya, Nelson and I were able to get four additional workers who were all mobile with either bicycles or cars and started to break up all the store locations amongst the lot of us to see what each team member would get.

Jasper told Tanya since she was so helpful and one of the original challenge team members, that she could keep all of the profits for anywhere she cleaned personally and they would split all of the commissions they received from the additional workers half and half.

As team leaders, Tanya and Jasper would each get three locations at $25 each, ten stores at $15 each and $5 commission from each of the forty-four stores the cleaners complete. The other four cleaners would get one store at $25 each and ten stores at $15 each with the understanding that they would give $5 of each payment to be split amongst Jasper and Tanya.

Tanya was so excited because up until now as part of her way of making the money for the challenge, she was reading stories to kids at a local library, but it only paid $20 per session. On average she would do about 3 stories a week and only get about $60. The following week she was able to make $80 but that was not going to help her generate enough money to get to her goals in one month, so with this additional job she would be able to attain her goals and was extremely excited to be on board.

Now that Tanya and Jasper had created their own cleaning company and had four workers, Jasper was able to call all the shop owners and managers to confirm everyone who would be in attendance and discuss that he would at the beginning of each week collect all payments up front. He spoke via speaker so that Tanya could write down all locations, prices and schedules.

If it all went well just in one week Jasper and Tanya would personally earn $225 each plus the Commissions from each team member which was about $220 but that would be split amongst the two of them making it a profit of $110 each so the first week as long as no one cancelled they were destined to make $335 each all in one week.

Not that it would be easy but in the end, it would be quite profitable.

Just like that, it was time for us to disperse but I knew they would do well especially since they created a protocol of a wake-up call for all the members including each other to see who would be able to make it for each day and confirm them or put someone in their place if necessary.

As long as they did not disappoint the clients this agency was the start of something amazing.

Men intrinsically do not trust new things that they have not experienced themselves.

Niccolo Machiavelli

CHAPTER EIGHT

SUNDAY - WEEK TWO

This morning I woke up to a shock, the new VR Station that we were all working hard to purchase was going to come out a whole week early which meant that by next Friday what was supposed to be the 3rd week into our challenge was now going to be the actual release week of the game.

On the bright side, I knew that everyone on the team had jobs and we were all functioning well but with the third week being right around the comer my excitement was dwindling.

I realized after seeing all the hard work that has been going into everyone's jobs and learning all of these lessons in reference to spending your money wisely, I was no longer sure that I wanted to purchase this game for full price with so much of my hard-earned money.

I thought it was time for us to have an emergency team meeting because I was wondering if anyone else was feeling the way that I was plus now that I knew the game was going to come out earlier I wanted to see how much money everyone was able to raise within the last 2 weeks.

I went downstairs to ask my mom if I could have some friends over for dinner. Although it was last minute she said sure, she just had to confirm with my dad who within five minutes responded to her and I with a firm yes.

I proceeded to call everyone and as we all spoke I had this gut feeling that things were about to change. Everyone seemed to be on board for coming over tonight and before I knew it the day flew by and it was 6 p.m.

We were all seated at my dinner table looking forward to my mom's food. Tonight she made a few of my dad's favorite naija dishes such as fufu (pounded yam), jollof rice (a tomato based rice full of spices), obe eja dindin (stew fish) and fried sweet plantain.

Although we all had different cultural backgrounds we were all fans of good food regardless of where it stemmed from. We did not say much during dinner because we were all too busy eating but after we all headed to the den and started to speak at the same time.

They wanted to know why I called an emergency meeting so I dove right into my thoughts and I asked them if they knew that the game was going to come out early. Most of them didn't and I also expressed to them how I did not want to spend all of my money on one game console.

To my surprise, they all felt the same but they also had the conflicting feelings of wanting to purchase the game because it was being advertised as the best console yet.

We did not know how to balance the two even the most successful of all of us being the babysitter club thus far did not want to spend all of their money on the game even though they made the money and then some within the last two weeks.

We all knew by now that the game would not retain its monetary value and started to brainstorm ideas as to how we can fix our issue.

Should we wait till the game comes out and someone else we know purchases it and ask to play with it or should we just buy it since this was our goal this whole time?

As we shot out ideas Jasper said the most genius thing which definitely had all of us thinking, his remark was "if only we could buy one to see if we liked it enough to keep it". Just like that, I started to put together an idea which would benefit all of us, my suggestion was how about we purchased one game console and split the cost amongst the 8th of us that would mean we would each easily contribute only $68.75 of our earnings. After purchasing the first game console we would all play with it and could either decide to play with the one we would put money towards or purchase their own.

Little did we know that Tanya's next question would become the base of our group. She asked: "where would we play the new VR Station console?" Would the console be at one person's house or travel to a different house each week or did we think it best to just pay to play it at a local arcade?

With that last statement, Lincoln jumped and asked why couldn't we just open up an official kids club where all of us could go to relax, play the game and think of other genius ideas which would help us generate money and not to mention spend time together.

We all loved this idea and after rounds of deliberating, we came to the conclusion that since I was the glue that brought us all together and had an empty basement maybe we could do it at my house.

This also led me to asking them why were we only limiting our clubhouse to each other? why don't we also let other kids from our schools who we've interacted with and got along with come over to play the game console as well.

Like an arcade, we could charge them a small fee, something like maybe thirty minutes of play time for $1 and from there also generate money off of the game console.

Everyone loved this idea so I paused our conversations to go and ask my parents if it would be possible for us to even utilize the basement, I realized it did not make sense for us to go any further if we did not have a space to use.

I found both my parents still in the kitchen cleaning up after all of us which was really cool of them usually that was my chore but because they knew we had an important meeting for tonight they let me slide on the dishwashing duty.

I asked my parents would it be possible for me to utilize our basement as a kid Clubhouse since it had a separate entrance and the kids from our neighborhood and schools did not have to actually come through the whole house to get to it and my dad's first question was what would be the purpose of us using the basement.

I explained to him how we were all "kidpreneurs" and that's kind of when it clicked to me that that should be the name of our group, we were a group of kids who were entrepreneurs. Our Kidpreneurs club would purchase only one VR Station console and play it amongst ourselves but as well make money from it by letting other kids play at a cheap cost.

My dad thought it was a great idea and my mom did too and proceeded to asks what would be the price point of the contribution per person for the game console and how would that split work if somebody decided later on that they wanted their own game console.

I explained the amount would be $68.75 per person and we would give them their $68.75 back if it has been less than a year and that led me to my next thought: since it would be in my own basement, if at the end of the month I wanted to keep the game, with their approval I would keep it and give each person back their $68.75 investment and take full ownership of the game. If not, we could discuss returning it or give it to another team member, etc.

With my parents' approval, I went back to the group and told them that we had our first official Club group space I also told him about how I thought we should call ourselves kidpreneurs since we all had our own small businesses.

Everyone thought it was a great idea and now the next step would have to be figuring out how much money would we put towards the electricity as well as what would we have in our clubhouse and how much would we invest each in making it become a reality.

This led to the next group of our excited discussions and we started to all formulate ideas and lists of things our clubhouse should have like a consulting comer and desk so we could all conduct business including a computer for research, two TV's and a big couch.

It was looking like we had a lot of work to do but it was going to be worth it.

Each generation must, out of relative obscurity, discover its mission, fulfill it, or betray it.

Frantz Fanon

CHAPTER NINE

FRIDAY - WEEK THREE

In just four days with help from our parents, our group was able to completely set up the kidpreneur clubhouse and plan our first event for Saturday.

We created a $5 per person entry fee with the understanding that if all went well we would have the new VR Station Console for them to play for at least thirty minutes.

Before we knew it by Thursday night we had thirty-two RSVPs and an inbox of teens from other schools inquiring about joining our kidpreneurs club.

By 8 am this morning my group of friends and I were officially proud owners of one new VR Station which is now located in our clubhouse. By 12 pm all of our rsvp guests were in attendance and having a blast. If you walked around the room you would hear kids scheduling their next visit or calling their friends and telling them about how cool our space was.

If someone told us that in just three weeks we would no longer want to purchase eight individual consoles or that our tunnel vision would be replaced with a yearning to spend our earnings wisely at all times we probably would've told them they were wrong.

What started out as a challenge to purchase eight VR Stations has transformed into the eight of us banding together and creating our own Kidpreneurs club.

After all of our guests went home our only concern was not getting enough time to play ourselves and we thought it best to add money towards purchasing one more console for our clubhouse.

One VR Station would only be for our group of kidpreneurs to play with and the other to be rented out to our guests.

We all agreed that this was the best summer ever thus far and we were all looking forward to continuing our jobs.

Thanks for following our journey and all that we have accomplished thus far.

To think, this is only the beginning...

Kidpreneurs: Wants vs Needs

Kidpreneurs: Wants vs Needs

Kidpreneurs: Wants vs Needs

Made in the USA
Middletown, DE
19 July 2020